Worth IT

Alicia Davis

BookLeaf Publishing

Presentation by *BookLeaf Publishing*

Web: www.bookleafpub.com

E-mail: info@bookleafpub.com

ISBN: 9789395088473

First edition 2022

DEDICATION

I get the chance to give back to my womb - My son Brayden

ACKNOWLEDGEMENT

I would like to thank My amazing partner and friend not to mention the best father in the world to our son Brayden- Thank you Brandon for proofreading my work and encouraging me to believe in me again and again :) whenever I handed you my laptop without asking you first.

PREFACE

This book is not about you if you don't want it to
be.
Although my poetry - my words and perspective
of life seems subjective
I want to remind you I too felt that this wasn't
about me.. when really it was always about me
and you.
no one accepts war but we want peace
well, what do you want?
Y. O. U.
count your birthday as something special
rub your dogs belly
listen to uncensored music
find the answers in a book
but what I W O N ' T tell you
is that this book is about you or me
THIS BOOK IS ABOUT WHAT'S INSIDE
YOU.

Anything Grows. (Period

I remember when I felt " like this" we all have
said that before.
Do you remember the exact time maybe what
you were wearing or even better how it made
you feel?
It was like my body could do nothing about what
was going on in my head.
in my own world foreign to the physical to the
present to the right now.
Everything MENTAL
I could not get out of my head
everything...
everything i thought about was a thought about
what i was thinking about.
Have you ever thought about that?
what?!
How had I gotten here?
I couldn't see anything with clarity look me in
my eyes on everything i've had days like that.
Drowning, losing, sinking, blending, forgetting,
and not learning or growing IMPOSSIBLE to
change- stuck.
I was becoming emotionally unstable.
How do you feel?
Lack of emotional intelligence

Uncertainty, scripted, not genuine, fighting,
kicking, screaming pinned up energy
suppressed.

And the remedy?

Live
LOVE
Laugh and be careful what you take in and what
comes out of your own head be Limitless and
remember anything grows and you are here.

Too much that's how much

Listen here son I'll tell you my love for you is
this much; as I proceeded to show him the
quantity of love measured with my hands.
He says: "too, too, much ?
The uncertain tone in his voice shook force in
my heart because I knew that showing was
better than telling.
Well, son it is never a time when I won't. I
thought about saying when do I not show you
love, but most importantly I felt what he wasn't
saying.

"Because the truth is there will be times when I
don't."

Like a mother lioness defending her cub I grab
him and we sink into laughter, crying, laughing,
and loving also - not understanding how
powerful the moment of facing our own truth
really is.

My son said see me and listen to me he spoke
those words to me frustrated but he was standing
in his own truth while questioning how
unworthy he could possibly be when his mother

yells at the top of her voice because of spilled
milk or when days at work have left mother
drained and uninterested in how to tie shoes.

 "Could you love me this much ? "

Brayden, I love you all the time there is no time
when I Won't but many times when I don't.
Could I quantify my mother's love for my son
when you smile I do too
when you wonder I question I promise I do.
You make me a better human for you and when
you need me I'll be there too.
If the world gets heavy and you can't seem to
make up your mind
as often as you say: "but I can't mommy ." I will
say: but what if you can ! ?
I am your gatekeeper your help and way
THROUGH .
We breathe and live to tackle another day of
kindergarten.

I think the mother in me finally understands that
love is subjective and my 6 year old like many
of us are wondering how much is too much ?

I live another day of motherhood to tell you that
our love as mothers or as women carrying
wombs last forever - many lifetimes over - love

is brave, love is patient and love is sometimes
understanding that no one not even our mothers
know everything- because love is endless and it
changes although plentiful it is painful.

How much is too much... we might never know,
but what we do know is that love, motherhood,
and children are all reflections of the realities we
create. We make choices every time we wake
and before we end our day we rest in the
imperfections and unquantifiable assurance that
too much is just enough.

Cup Filled.

What it means to be filled is a matter of how you
look at the cup
who's looking at the cup is secondary and just as
stressful alright enough!
" I had to get out of my own head."

It's not always about being seen as much as it is
about seeing yourself inside out the fortune
cookie read.

So, I went to see a man about a dog about my
cup and the therapist said:
"who are you? "

"Don't give me anything that can fit inside a
cup."

It was a matter of how she said it and not what
she said in the many therapy sessions of life :
salon chairs
car talks
bathroom banter
OR
auntie Rita's house

I started a journal entry trying to attach meaning
to the newest journey I was embarking upon and
shortly after I had failed myself again.
Not consistent with anything and my biggest
flex was my inability to hold my own feet to the
fire. I disappointed myself looking for an excuse
when there was none.
My moment of self doubt: how small would I
need to be to fit inside a cup Subjecting my life
experiences to a three letter word.
I responded well in the midst of my melt down
one of my favorite persons called
I got inspired to be vulnerable to let go of what I
feel to actually see what reality I was creating.

Bingo... the textbook answer... now what's next ?

Have you ever thought about the things you do
to reap the results you desire?

Present in the moment of my life's drama I
realized that every thought actualized or
repeated negative and positive belonged to me.

I didn't finish the assignment on time, but I did
complete it.
Hoping to be appeased by the mere fact that I
had showed up and how grateful People should
feel to be in the presence of me.

Holding out my cup and never filling anyone
else's up.

In & Out

She was in and out of it a lot probably her whole
life now.
How had she ever got through, she uttered to
herself.
Crying one day merciless in her suburban mom's
attic car
she was in and out of it.
It was then but then again had been so many
times before.
How can the ego be good and bad she thought to
herself?
Going through countless screenshots and papers
put away in a box in a closet looking through
any message where she may have mentioned
something that mattered to her something that
was scared and sacred.
She was in and out. ..had been here a time
before.
last lifetime her life had been the worst survival
movie with facial captions:
[We not making it out of this, this is f**** crazy,
I can't believe this is happening, this can't be my
life and I can't live like this] !
selfish
selfish

selfish
selfish selfish fears for myself.
she was in trouble and out of options
she was in "a changing period of her life and she
wanted out."
she was me
I identified that my ego and inability to maintain
balance in my life was crushing me,
everyone around me
everything inside me
Nothing that grows stays the same.
You can't say that she didn't want to change or
didn't want to do better.
{achieve anyway }
locked in mentally.
Cccearly reading between the lines
protecting the physical glory of something not
actualized.
She was in and out
It all came back to this:
there was no question about certain things and
yet she questioned
there was no wonder about the simple things and
yet she wondered
worry.
Panic
Pain
Injury
accident

scare
fear
FREEDOM
Through and through must we all go
She was growing through what she needed to get
through
She was in and out.

Mother May I

Mother may I be
"How exactly do you mean child? "
"The way I would need to be given I can be me."
I can be me right mama?
Child in this world you can't just be.
You have to be Intentional
Be careful Be courteous.
Creative cute mute.
I couldn't believe she said be silent during the
storm as she has said times and times before.
You can't always speak up, but mother (listen
girl !) just wait til your turn
it ain't your turn to shine.
You may be a woman and you may have these
dreams but you have to make a living.
"You work ."
{Interrupting}:
be smart - Ma ?
"hard you need" ?
This the only way.
Blinded at even the possibility of having an
answer she said i've thought about it
the room fell silent.

I didn't defend myself I didn't defend my dreams
I submitted to her expectations of me and got
back in line.
MOTHER may I please ?

If You Don't Look

Why can't they see me ?
It's all about the psychology
material shit.

Frequencies and black holes
9 suns came from black mothers and according
to our ancestors.
We are waiting for you.

Energy cannot be destroyed.
It is transferred through our interactions.
We must return to love.
re=turn to nature
be careful of what depletes and leaves us

This or that.
Left or right.
Up or down.
Front or behind
 ? you ?
us >> them
Nature or cut from consciousness.

Why do you think they are looking at me ?
Do you think they know about me?

Why are you always questioning yourself?
Is it because you fear the truth?

love me.
learning more about me.
I am me and if you don't look you will never see
the true me.
look inside and find the me that is also you.

I am because...

look at me
not with what meets the eye but see me through
and through
search my heart through truth
confront me with care and character
when you speak to me speak your truth
see my flaws and my glows
forgive yourself first then forgive others
there is etiquette in loving me
when you speak on my family you speak on me
when you isolate and separate Africa you take
from me
I'll take the sweet and the sour
the duality that is good and bad
different directions all leading me to where my
spirit wants to be
I am because they once were: my ancestors
wildest dreams
my parents connection and my family's rise
against it all
can tell you tragedies and triumphs
because as the sun rises it also sets and if it rains
its bound to shine
98 % of who I am is because I am

because.... I don't expect you to understand or respect but know that I exist and I'm not going anywhere... and again and time again I am because.

Not another love song

It can't be the same tune playing in my head but
it is
the same style, rhythm, and cadence I can feel it
it's coming the moment of truth... the moment
when I grow up
the moment that I either tell the truth or lie
I had been preparing for this moment
Can you believe I was falling in and out of love
?
synchronicity I can't explain a step to pain and a
beat to depression
Knocking down emotions un heald freshly
packed together get ready for Combustion a
chemical reaction to the bullshit built up inside
This cant be another love song
I don't have room to man up for the man I want
in my life.
Being too strong for far too long.
Reward comes to those who cry and now it's
time to wash away the guilt erase the
Frustrations of things not adding up and the
small possibility
Pretty Dreamers subtract.
Left: fractions of a women saying,
Not another love song

Damaged goods.
Be careful with me!
Staring at the 50 word text and how I turned a simple question about where you wanna eat tonight into world war 3 is beyond me.
This love isn't perfect neither is it void of love songs and cliche moments.
Real and that's simply not another love song.

Dear Diary Entry 222*

Imagine different days.
Dreams full of fulfilled fun.
Bad vibes blindsided by the fact that we really
don't have beef.
We see the world different we see life and the
right to live it the same way when We are
together.
I wan't often imagining doing life without you.
 I once said and you know what he said, nothing,
but what he did up close
I wake:
remembering how it felt: eyes locked inside
love, we shared this moment.
Telling me everything I needed to know by the
way he handled my feelings.
I never want to let go
It was those moments and we had them often,
and as much as I knew he was making me better.
I often entertained letting him go.
never felt the same even as I imagined because
letting go was a hard thing to do physically.
Dear Diary, I never want to let this man go
so here we are: you stay and I stay
imagine this day everyday just because we treat
each other better each day.

Well Wishes and wants for all things better
I hope one day you get to read this letter.
Good for one another each one teaching one.
We never even imagined having a son and he is
a perfect combination of how we both have
loved each other.
Only thoughts of you gets me by.
I wouldn't die for you, but I would live for you
and i hope you feel the same way 222

Daydream

As my favorite Lupe Fiasco song"Daydream"
plays in my head, I become aware.
woken by the harsh reality and sleep throughout
the fantasy that is life.
blinded by choices we often make it is now that
I acknowledge my truth.

Bothered by the ideas consuming my personality
and who I truly wanted to be
I realized for the first time I was daydreaming.
living in a memory world thinking of all the
ways I can't do or won't do
while, agreeing to negative production and lack
of change
what are the chances that I fly ?
Could I believe in me - rooting for me
somewhere deep inside was my control -my
destiny.
Illuminated as a constant reminder to look
forward and no longer in the past for
The need to succeed must be rooted in change
and growth.
We can no longer stay the same we must meet
our match through intentional and experiences
we decide to make best out of.

Down the stretch it will be nothing like we imagined but everything we are prepared for.
There are voices we know and past lives we have lived.
There is a silence so loud it brings us to tears and a womb so wide we fear enter ALONE.
So we daydream...
Never accepting, adopting, actualizing, true autonomy
The next LEVEL is something we can feel and everything that we do is about that mission - a journey it is and a time to be alive.

Black Blues

The right to do what I know to be right is my
right.
what rights does a black man have if he has no
rights ?
to be black can bring the blues
to be black means just like me or you
to be black is a song I hold in my heart
I carry Blackness concealed so afraid and
sometimes scars of the world from within
black out and black pride or black brown and
black sad.
How does being black look to you?
Maybe it was being accused of not paying for
everything I left the store with that day.
It could be that when a tall man walks by and his
hoodie is masking his face still.
Doesn't hide that he's black and that i may be
afraid
If you know me then you know my black is
really a grey stone boarded in the middle of the
block.
We were family even after the block
Ghetto enough to get and smart enough to know
that when we want out we put out.

Do you hear those cries of joy praising that boy
because he made it out the NeighborHOOD a-
precious life he can actually live; baby girl aka
mook who goes to school in cowboy boots AND
A SHORT SKIRT - IT'S WASHING DAY AND
SHE GONE TO SCHOOL ANWAY.
Don't talk about our values: we smile when its
hard and laugh to keep from crying
I am black Blues you and me through and
through
Can't wash away this stained soot of a look it's
written all over my face.
This is Black.
This is my blue hope I didn't blow you.

Therapy

"You are who you say you are."
You make agreements everyday.
"That's the thing... I'm not ."
Sometimes I don't know if i'm coming or going
"So you question? "
If my life is what it should be
& i'm here to make a difference, but god I am
trying.
I have been sheltered from a lot and it hurts
saying I don't know
"You won't know everything right ? "
It's possible that I feel pressured to know I can
agree with that
I also know that learning what I don't know is a
process
This is my first time here and I seem to want to
escape anything new
"But You can; if you lend yourself to something
you go with it."
If you don't...?
"Everything comes back to you.

Excuses

Excuses!
I don't
I can't
I won't
Affirm: you mean to be present
the truest hearts desires are framed through
action
Do you Honestly believe people can Change?
"I do."
I commit to the fantasy of how others respond to
me
giving myself much power and soon after
realizing what I carry and what I feel
consumes what I project and how I show up!
i. i. i. i. i. i
Excuses !
Often to others changing even before I commit
myself to me and just maybe before it all falls
down.
Excuses!
Through the lens of self you don't know what
people see
You can feel the vibrations of your inner self;
deeper versions of who you imagine To be...
ultimately becoming he/ she/ it/ having what you

think you want and most of what you actually except for.
Excuses!
You can, can care less about what your going through or grow through you moods and center your sassy side.
Pulling yourself aside to see another picture not the one you paint inside your head Atop a body that needs to pay it more attention!
Are you listening?
I'm talking to YOU
miss judgment.
 passing prejudgements.
getting over the offense of past judgements.
I am done making an excuse for why I haven't begun.
In the skin i'm in I need.

Boy. Hair. Love. Repeat.

I owe my son an apology.
several not nows' and i'll think about it to avoid
an emotional rollercoaster.
"Son your hair is beautiful let me show you.
He grabs hair wincing with pain as I pull -
tugging (ouch, "he screams !") with as much
force to get the job done and enough authority to
bounce back his coils.
"How are they wearing it now", I say to myself,
springy, greased and maintained as I Model him
around the mirror bathroom.
My Boy's hair has a nature of its own.
If HE treats it well and willing becomes a pot of
coily-curly manageable hair
HAIR LOVE the kind that my black boy needed.
Homegrown as I think of all the ways to make
him see pride in self.
In the final pressure stages he makes his
presence complimenting himself in the mirror
irritated about the process.
"Mom, it's not nappy ? "
"No son."
 Beautiful not nappy.

Saving Souls

It's something about the mystique of the lord that
I finally understand
mysterious ways mysterious blessings and
sometimes mysterious hands.
I finds myself thinking what did that even mean
smiling deeply inside with every quiver my
upper lip gives like when i'm lying to get ahead
or stepping on the necks of my haters because it
feels good to be understood. I remember laying
on the thighs of my grandmother as she shook
her leg furiously unsatisfied and often irritated.
It was something in her spirit a fight that was
solemn and centered it evoked praise and
worshiped and so I proceeded to bow to the
knees of my maker
the mother of all mothers my grandmother.
Grandma had feet that felt like paper cuts and
sandy beaches. The blessed oil was smooth and
seemed to consume every crack. With an even
distribution she was satisfied. I then wanted
grandma to bless me with one of her songs an
old hymn. she seemed to put on the best
dramatic calls to God when our family needed.

she was saving our soul.

That meant soul food at funerals and less
worrying even in the midst of crying. Then
there's something alluring about the way she
went to sleep. Never a quiet room, but a space
full of prayers and peace. She was good for the
soul. Like your favorite song, my grandma could
make you laugh when you really wanted to hide
from the fears of the world. Spiritually gifted
with a third eye for feeling when it was time for
change. I often think about how she felt leaving
us all behind. Maybe she didn't know that she
would no longer inhabit the body that I oh so
adored. Afterall the shell of her existence was
not in her skin,but in her voice. I can still hear
how she laughed over a full moon and still hear
the clanging of pot and pan preparing a sunday
meal. some things just don't change embedded in
my heart like a tattoo, yet taboo like wanting to
grow but never accepting change.

she was saving my S. O. U. L >>

Heroes

Waiting for no one we countdown. Superman where are you?
Have you recently forgot that we belong to you too?
There is a man that knows everyone and everyone knows him and for this reason they call him super they call us man and we are his children. Mr. everybody can we come to thee unafraid and accepting of the things we know not? Is there a list checking us off one by one or should we hide from the universe under the stars.
We have been before a very long time ago and now is the time that we become Super.
 3, 2, 1... we take off going about the busy lives we have been assigned. Fall in line to take a piece of what was rationed for all. Running ,raging, rambling rescue us! You asked if we've been waiting and time has been moving all along as birthdays indicate how we live our life day after day. We are told to prepare for the end but we are already there. Awakened from within beginning all over again and again. How long have we been sleeping? Functioning in a state of dysfunction alternatively pressing through

what we think we can call our truth. These were
the times our ancestors predicted. Drunken with
wine on the days we want to forget and so it is
said that we create our own realities. Agreeing
socially on what is accepted and rejected. I
wrote many songs Unsung and told a couple
lies: life undone. If I can go back and remember
who had come before me... what do you imagine
I would see?

Letting Go

I had to let it all go.
one day I sat on the side of the bed knowing that
it was time to say goodbye.
To progress in the moments not my best is to
dress up a hot mess. girl let it go!
My hips get wider and my shoe size has gotten
bigger it's time to pass on what no longer fits. As
I sort through old clothing i've held onto, its
evident that choosing what to wear has masked
my true identity. Shirts and pants memories
cloud my view- all different characters i've
portrayed. Clothes big and way too small I begin
to ball them up to throw Away. Not erasing the
memories yet preparing for a new fit.

F. L. Y. - First Love Yourself

The girl sat at her desk with her head down her
spirit sank even lower in her chair shoulders
filled with desperation and exhaustion.
often in her head a lot boxed in with the thought
of keeping what no longer serves her out and yet
still perplexed about how to move forward. This
was the ways of the world and her first lesson
and looking at everything as a lesson to learned.
she was figuring it out while being teachable and
learning that love can sometimes hurt especially
when you don't give enough to yourself. We all
can identify with that girl. Smiling while hurting
inside. Playing it cool as emotions often run high
leaving a facial expression that serves a cold
room its own reflection. She's not always
determined needing her village to lift her up and
see to it she belongs where she was planted
blooming through a gloomy day or aligning her
destiny by giving of herself unselfishly. To be
the best me I can possibly be means looking
beyond me. Self is a prideful thing and even this
world sees human as single alone. The question
then becomes to whom do I belong and to what
do I owe ? Can the world handle all of me ? Can
I rise above the many expectations put on me ?

My grandmother would always say anything worth having doesn't come easy.
 Faith is the substance of things hoped for and the action behind every reaction.
 Our deepest fears is to create a New path that not only helps others, but helps us just the same. In a world controlled by keeping up with the Joneses what will we do next?

Animal v.s. You

You are wild and yet you are here
you are body yet you still hear
you are figure with the agility and ability to
adapt
Steadfast: unmovable.
Resilient and sloth like, but still rising like the
morning sun
Who is it that you may be?
Leader of your tribe passing through the beings
that are here just like you
Participant in the midnight sky making way for
the mile high journey to the new you.
God has blessed you with more than you have
asked.
It sits well with you to do good for others as you
would yourself.
God with thought of transcending into the
unknown.
You can be what you can see.
Hemmed up against the external pressures and
so you adopt all around you
making and molding what they said you couldn't
do.
Fearing that you are closer to your dreams than
in reality it may seem unbecoming

You become and yet anyway like stillness in
light you burst into many versions of another
self for the end in in sight.
parading through the kingdom as predators often
do hoping you wont get eaten while eating to
survive is something you must do.
Trying to be of the purest intentions your actions
will get you through only if you learn to lead by
the need to transcend.
You must know your place in order to pass on
something great.
Intangible is what you can't see, but what you
feel an inner knowing that you are transforming.

History is not Her: Story

I am a new mother.
I believe I was led to this moment as a caregiver,
a nurturer and a representative from my past.
I am black woman.
Strongly convinced that my love is a struggle
and fight, I lay my worries down lowering my
expectations every time I feel unprepared.
The world is breaking me. the world is against
me please release me from who i'm supposed to
be.
She and others building me up through
sisterhoods and small wins,
I hope my baby sister and my mother remember
we carry the same seeds.
Our stories often untold so we grow old with
disgust and mistrust.
We were the chosen ones we were left behind
and it is me who is speaking up for
all of us.
With child i've taken on more responsibility than
a job I am expected to know.
Reframing from my head a list of do rights and
to sometimes go with
FRUSTRATIONS

I've learned that all comes through mother and I am new to this hoping to become true to this body + mind + soul.
Holding onto the tangible fixed nature that is not truly me because who I imagine to be is a combination of who I am when God is within me.
This is my story to tell and although there is so much withheld I am listening and yearning to learn how exactly I came to be.
Darling open your eyes.

The beginning is the end if you choose

Grace allows self to be fearless and still to grow through what you go through
peace gives yourself all the time and patience to learn something new everyday and love accepts the things you simply cannot change and decides to be You anyway. How sweet it is to come from the womb ready to leave a lasting impression. Who can this You be and how can you get there are questions that will run the course as long as the mind remains free. You can be limitless if you choose and everything that happens under the sun is also protected and guided by the forces that are: the sun, the moon, the dust, the dirt, the water, and the air is all life that we must see internally. Each level I expect to rise above the physical and learn to swim amongst the spiritual. There is pain and progress in struggle but most importantly there is a song in my voice and a mountain top it has yet to reach.